MW01518263

My Naked Self

MY POETRY : MY HEART & SOUL

Thanks for my Peace of Mind

Brigitte Cinq-Mars

BRIGITTE CINQ-MARS

authorHOUSE®

AuthorHouse™
1663 Liberty Drive
Bloomington, IN 47403
www.authorhouse.com
Phone: 1-800-839-8640

© *2009 Brigitte Cinq-Mars. All rights reserved.*

No part of this book may be reproduced, stored in a retrieval system, or transmitted by any means without the written permission of the author.

First published by AuthorHouse 9/3/2009

ISBN: 978-1-4389-7539-9 (e)
ISBN: 978-1-4389-7537-5 (sc)
ISBN: 978-1-4389-7538-2 (hc)

Library of Congress Control Number: 2009906669

Printed in the United States of America
Bloomington, Indiana

This book is printed on acid-free paper.

Page of Dedication

To my parents who ingrained in me the values of love, kindness,
honesty, strength and independence.
To all who knowingly or unknowingly helped me evolve
in mind, body and spirit; family, friends, aquaintances
and sometimes complete strangers.
Especially to my love and inspiration, Kevin;
thankyou for your unwavering confidence and support,
and thankyou for allowing me to always be
my naked self.

Table Of Contents

Chapter One : How Do I Love Thee

Chapter Two : Songs of My Youth

Chapter Three : My Limitations

Chapter Four : Suffering and Solice

Chapter Five : My Passion and Purpose

Chapter Six : What I've Learned

Chapter Seven : Dawn Has Broken

Chapter Eight : Faith and Philosophy

Chapter Nine : Good Wishes

Chapter 1 :
How Do I Love Thee

Unconditionally

I love you unconditionally
There is no bad or good, right or wrong
There is simply you
Whomever you choose to be
Whatever you choose to do
You are perfect as you are
You need not try to "live up" to anything
Open your eyes and you'll realize
That you're already there
You've always been
If you wish to change, to grow,
Don't hesitate
You will still be just as perfect
You cannot be more perfect
You can choose to be different than who you were before
I will love you All ways, forever.

Soulmates

I love you with every atom of my being
It matters not if you're my friend, lover, sister or parent
You are in my life that's all I care
No greater peace will I ever find than knowing this
We need not be together all the time
Although there is no greater joy than to be near you
My soul rejoices simply knowing we breath the same air
If you should leave this world and I should stay,
Come back to me, we'll start anew
You can be my son, my daughter,
Or whomever you choose
It matters not who you decide to be
I will recognize your eyes, your smile,
Souls never forget and never let go
Life after life we'll meet for the first time
Each time we'll say "I feel like I've known you forever"
It's our soul's way of saying "It's so nice to see you again!"

Marriage

Two souls choosing to come together in union
To gain strength from each other
Without either trying to overpower the other
To grow together
Without either expecting the other to change
If change does occur
Accepting each other still
Loving each other all the more
Choosing to be faithful to one and other
Because just the thought
Of causing their loved one pain
Is unbearable
Feeling each others' sorrow or joy as their own
Maintaining their individuality always
Yet choosing to experience life together.

A Soft Place To Fall

You are my soft place to fall my love
No matter what challenges life brings
Coming home to you reminds me
Why I work till I can't focus
Smile when I'd rather scream
Stay positive when giving up would be so much easier
And laugh when I want to cry
You inspire me to be strong yet soft
Brave as well as vulnerable
Calm yet passionate
Because of you I have learned
To laugh at myself and my troubles
Enjoy every moment we share
And thank God for my many blessings
The greatest of which is you

Through all of my life's trials and tribulations
When I thought God had abandoned me
I was told I expected too much out of life
That I was a dreamer
Then you came along
And gave me a soft place to fall
Never giving up on me
Always standing by me
Then you look at me with amazement
And tell me You're the lucky one
Thankyou for letting me fall into your arms
When I had no strength left
Believing in me when no one else did
And being my light when all else was dark
My faith is restored
For you are my gift, my angel,
My soft place to fall

Friends

What defines a friend?
Should there be conditions or parameters?
Does each individual have their own opinions
Of what those parameters should be
Or how a friend should or should not behave?
If we concentrated our efforts on how to be a good friend
Instead of scrutinizing other's efforts to be ours,
We would attract the like.
My definitions are simple:
I will treat you with respect and dignity,
I will be by your side when you grieve,
I will rejoice in your happiness.
I need not see or hear from you
For days, months, or even years,
My elation will be equally great
With each reunion.
I will help you fight your demons
If that is what you ask
Or sit by your side in silence
If a quiet presence is what you need.
You have my confidential trust
Till the day that you break mine.
If such a day arrives,
The time for friendship ends.
I wish you well in life
But you are no longer welcome in mine.

Children

The greatest blessing of all.
A soul that chooses to start a new life through us
It is truely a privilege and a gift.
We have a responsibility to guide them
Without restricting their choice of path.
To discipline yet not punish.
Praising them for their every effort
While teaching them there is no such thing as failure,
Only learning experiences.
Sometimes difficult ones,
But always valuable.
Help them to know and feel that love is limitless;
Understanding the most wonderful experience
Is giving love.
Only then are we completely fulfilled.
If this be all we are able to teach a child,
We have taught them the secrets of the universe.
Love reunites the most disconnected of souls.
For it is the essence of who and what we are.
Children re-instill this in us.
They come into our lives to remind us of
The purity of love,
That we are born perfect.
Just as we see the beauty and perfection in them,
They see it in us.

Chapter Two : Songs of My Youth

Mother

Mother where are you now?
You were here for so many years
But now you're gone

Mother where are you now?
You were slowly fading away
And now your gone

Please won't you pray for me?
I'm scared to see what the future
Has in store for me

Mother can you hear what they're saying?
They're telling me not to care like I do
They're telling me not to worry
But I can't seem to understand
They're telling me I'm just like you

Mother can you see me now?
Am I making you proud?
You know I've always wanted to

Mother can you see me now?
I'm living my dream
Just like I've always wanted to

Mother please pity me
I still have my foolish pride
What am I to do?

Mother can you hear what I'm saying?
Be reassured I still remember you
Mother how I've missed you
It's been oh so hard without you
Mother, I will always love you.

I Make the World go Around

I am blind yet I see all
I am weak yet the strongest of all
I hurt when I'm alone
But when I'm two
That's when I'm strong
For I am Love
And I make the world go around

I am shy yet I am bold
I am the story that's often told
I last forever yet not so long
And when I'm gone
You can't carry on
For I am Love
And I make the world go around

I am not just a game
Yet I'm a gamble just the same
I need no fortune or fame
Yet I receive them
Just the same
For I am Love
And I make the world go around

I can touch and I can feel
What's in your heart I will reveal
You cannot see me but I'm there
Your heart of stone
Will start to care
For I am Love
And I make the world go around

Hamlet's Theme

Living or dying
Confusion is flying
Questions outnumber
The answers evasive

Why? Tell me why
The children cry
The parents lie
The pain sets in
The soul distraught
Escape is sought
From this one son

Mother how could you treat father that way?
Adulteress with his brother
You killed him you bitch!
You conniving scheming witch!
My sweet loving mother...
You are no more!

Clever were you
Put poison in his ear
Who would ever hear
Of such a crime?
So liethal the drops
They burnt right through his brain
You've got to be insane
Or am I...?

16

There's no such thing as ghosts
Everybody knows it
Does everybody know it?
Or have you really risen from the dead
My dear old dad?

You want revenge!
Must you get it through me?
Is it really you?
Or am I going crazy?

And what about my love?
I must keep her out of this
How shall I tell...

My sweet Ophelia
Lord knows I love you
But you must go away
For I am not the man you use to know
I cannot give you an explanation
You must simply stay away from me

For a man's got to do
What a man's got to do
And if it brings me to my end
Then so shall it be

Ode to Terry Fox

God we need a man
Who'll carry this world upon his shoulders
And bring it to a better place and time
Someone who'll show us
How to love one and other
Someone who'll teach us how to care

There was such a man
His dedication unified a nation
The passion for the cause
Must live on in us all
We need a man like Terry once again

He moved to tears the most cynical people
The jaded and sophisticated
Though pity and compassion not his goal
The rarest of courage
Endless determination,
Terry Fox, an inspiration to all

Have we forgotten
What he was fighting for?
The marathon of hope
Has yet to be completed
We must stand together and carry on

Somehow the pain must stop
Somehow the hurting must end
Together we can do it
I know we've got the spirit
Oh Canada take pride and carry on

Chapter Three : My Limitations

A Line In The Sand

It has been said that we teach people how to treat us,
That forgiveness is not about the other person,
It is about our own peace of mind.
If we are to avoid abuse,
Whether verbal, emotional, physical, or neglectful,
We must each draw a line in the sand.
I will forgive much,
But this does not mean I will tolerate it.
Lashing out in the heat of the moment
Is unacceptable.
We always have a choice;
Being angry is no excuse for hurting another.
I will forgive such behavior,
However if someone demonstrates
That they are capable of such,
I choose not to have them
In any part of my life.
Negativity and anger are like a disease;
If you allow it in any part of your life,
It will infect all of your life.
If there is a choice between hurting another or not,
There should be no choice.
If you believe there is,
You have crossed my line in the sand.
If that be the case,
Then have a nice life
But stay out of mine.

No Time

No time to write
No time to read
Too busy working
To remember to breath
Rushing to meet responsibilities
Organizing our scheduals
To make time to please
Leaving us little time for our own ease
Worries consume almost all of our time
Time is short, time is precious
Live for the moment
For we can only go forward
And time flies by faster than light
Live consciously, with purpose
For there's no time to waste
Our own time can end
While we think and wait

Tired Days

Even optimists have tired days,
When every breath is one deep sigh after another.
I'm so busy keeping everyone up
I run out of steam and get run down.
When a seemingly endless series of challenges
Tests my ability to keep on smiling
When there is so much small stuff
That it starts to feel like
A big wad of gum stuck to my shoe,
And the world can't seem to find any place to rest
Other than on my shoulders,
I just want to sleep
And wake up when the storm is over
Or till someone volunteers
To carry the burden.
So forgive me if I'm not so perky,
I'm just having a few tired days

Limbo

My enthusiasm for life has not waned,
Yet I feel like a mouse on a running wheel.
I know where I want go,
I know what I want to accomplish,
My goals are clear.
There is no doubt in my mind
What needs to be done.
My frustration lies
In the seemingly endless obstacles in my way.
Although my happiness is not compromised,
These obstacles are wearing.
Forever waiting
For the next stage of my life to begin.
Finding a new home,
Selling the old one,
Packing and painting and endlessly waiting
For work to be finished and decisions to be made.
If only I could wake up when all this is done,
This living in limbo is really no fun!
Alas such is life:
The work and the waiting
Are worth it in the end,
But the limbo in between
Might drive me around the bend!

Simplicity

My needs are simple or so I thought.
Yet for simple needs their achievement is not.
We strive for different versions of the same ends;
That complications and obstacles are done with
To achieve some sort of rythm in our life again.
I know life has it's challenges,
It's not always easy.
I just want to move forward,
Not sideways or back.
Never was good at line dancing,
Never had the desire to keep up with the pack.
Speaking of pack that is what I must do
For my road to simplicity is far from through.
So with these few words I bid you adieu:
May your life be simple,
Whatever simple may be to you.

Respect

You can command it,
You can demand it,
You can expect it,
But until you give it,
You will never earn it,
Much less receive it.
What is respect?
It is using good manners,
It is being polite,
It is listening to someone
Without interupting.
It is unfortunately in todays society
Quickly becoming a lost art.
Please and thankyou
Will soon become part of an ancient language.
Respect means behaving in a manner
That reflects how you prefer to be treated;
With grace and dignity.

Chapter 4:

Suffering and Solice

Angry Words

Why would you trust anyone's word over mine
When all I've always been is honest to a fault?
Why would you be so disrespectful
When I have treated you with grace and dignity?
Why would you be jealous of my happiness
When all I ever wanted for you was joy?
Why would you say such hurtful things
Just to win an arguement
When even in my frustration,
I would rather die silently than cause you pain?
Why would you think I'm out to get you
When I've always been your most loyal supporter?
Why would you direct all of your anger towards me
When all I ever did was love you with all my heart?
Why would you deny your own pain
When your actions make it obvious?
What are you afraid of?

Sorrow

Sorrow is the most difficult emotion to describe
Being separated from a beloved soul
Whether by distance or by death
Is like joyfully frolicking through life
Then suddenly tripping and falling down a well.
There is the initial shock of tripping
Followed by the awareness that you're falling
Then physical pain when you hit bottom
Feeling your soul being ripped apart
You awaken alone in the dark
You hear voices but no one can reach you
It's a long grueling climb back to the light
Some are not successful
Those who are help others
Feel the warmth of the sun once again
What is the purpose of all of this?
If we do not experience sorrow,
We cannot appreciate true joy.

Death

If death is seen as an ending of life,
Than death does not exist
For life is eternal.
It does not end,
It simply changes form.
The spirit expands
Beyond the body's ability to contain it.
In this instant,
The body is left behind.
It is the soul's most difficult task
To conform itself to
The limitations of the human body.
It chooses to do so
For it is an opportunity
To create life anew.
It is the soul's greatest challenge.

Death is not an ending to life
It is a transition
From a limited existence
To a limitless existence.
When the soul accomplishes
All that it intends
It simply continues the cycle
Experiencing the freedom of limitless expansion,
The re-membering of the soul group.
Then the excitement of creation once again.
The challenge of new beginnings,
What is called death,
Is actually the most joyous experience of Life.

Divorce

Without a doubt the most painful human experience
Overshadowing the loss of a loved one through death.
When someone you love dies
They do not leave you by choice;
You feel empty, lost and sometimes abandonned,
But the knowledge that they loved you
Till they're dying breath
Is reassuring even in your darkest hour.
The devastation of divorce
Is a direct attack to your selfworth.
Someone to whom you've given your heart and soul
Doesn't want them anymore,
Doesn't want you anymore.
You are not worth their time or effort.

The person you loved the most left you
Because they find something about you
Impossible to live with.
Family and friends often choose sides,
Sometimes leaving you with neither.
It is both crushing and terrifying.
You are left to rebuild your entire life
As well as your ego.
Just when you thought you had everything figured out,
You have to start all over again.
It is however a blessing in disguise;
You find strength you never knew you were capable of,
The return or discovery of your independance,
And a chance for a new beginning.
You become the butterfly,
Morphing into a new, stronger, wiser you

Silence Speaks Louder Than Words

How do you help a troubled soul?
Your own to teach is never ending
To sit and watch anothers turmoil
Bound and gagged, a hapless victim
Your ears, their only comfort
Like a babe in arms
Your heart is a cradle
Cornered, frightened
Tortured and snared
Lashing out, grasping blindly
And you still bound, still mute
Your heart, your sight
The only witness to the desperate cry
Silence speaks louder than words

Kind Words

It's amazing what a kind word can do
To uplift a soul who's tired and blue.
When I'm worn out from work
And I'm stressed out because
Life is a race
Of which I'm in third place.
Super mom, super friend,
Super woman till the end.
An image I fought for,
But now and again,
The respect that I longed for
Comes with worries that I'm in
Over my head
Oh where to begin!
Just a little more effort,
Just one more push,
If I can make it through this day
The next will be good.
Every kind word
Is fuel for the soul
They keep me going
When I'm on a roll

Kindred Spirits

Faraway friends
Never having met
Kindred spirits
Co-miserate and yet
Two different lives
And several hundred miles
Cannot prevent
The comfort that is met
Knowing that someone
Understands your fret.

<u>*Forgiveness*</u>

We have all been hurt.
We have all been offended.
Whether the offences were intended or not,
Matters not
For forgiveness is not about the offender,
It is about moving forward
Instead of stagnating.
Forgiving is making the most of the present
Instead of wasting precious time
Dwelling in the past.
What is done
Is done and gone.
You cannot change what has already happened.

More often than not
The offender is oblivious
To the crime in question
Or the pain that was caused.
Even when the offense was intentional
It is forgotten almost immediatly.
You cannot grow if you don't let go.
If we choose to harbor every offence inflicted on us
There is no room left in our hearts for love or joy;
Instead, our hearts fill with bitterness
Until we are completely consumed by it.
The best revenge is a happy life,
It is choosing not to take offense,
Realizing words only have value
If you give them worth.

Menopause

The end of reasoning,
The beginning of reason.
Through our teens and twenties
We're officially adults
So don't try to tell us what to do or how to do it,
We believe we know everything.
The trial and error phase
When we're invincible
And it's all about us.
Then come the sacrificial thirties,
We're mature and responsible now;
We decide we'll take care of everyone
Sacrificing our own comforts
And setting aside our childhood dreams
To become the dependable ones.
It is a time of both humility and pride.
After having given ourselves completely
To our family and friends for the past decade
We realize we've made everyone happy but us.

The forties and fifties give us the wisdom of menopause.
We re-discover our own comforts and childhood dreams,
Learning to combine the carefree selfloving nature
Of the teens and twenties
With the strength and perserverance of the thirties,
Finally discovering our true natures.
Finding joy, happiness and peace of mind,
Realizing how precious and fleeting life really is,
And making the most of every moment,
Because decades pass in the blink of an eye
And yesterday we were only twenty.

Chapter Five : My Passion and Purpose

<u>*Work*</u>

The most important factor
That teaches each of us the responsibility of adulthood.
Those who don't enjoy their chosen profession
Call it a necessary evil.
To them it is a means to an end;
Putting in their time,
Waiting for retirement.
Others who have suffered without it,
Call it a blessing;
Appreciating the comforts of life it brings,
Never taking it for granted.
But when you love what you do
Your work becomes your passion,
Your calling,
Work becomes pleasure.
You enjoy your life while you're living it.
If you've experienced it once,
You'll settle for nothing less.

The Esthetician

People come and go,
Talking of their joys and sorrows.
I am the keeper of confidences
They arrive tired, weary and usually rushed
Feeling unattractive and unappreciated
As I tender loving care
I encourage them to vent
Knowing some have no other
I listen and acknowledge their every word
I give them a refuge and respite
From the trials and tribulations of their daily lives
A place where they can be their naked selves
They cry, they laugh, they let off steam
They release, relax and rejuvenate

When they leave their load is lightened
They're able to see and feel
What is obvious to me
The beauty that is inside and out
I am an esthetician
I don't make people beautiful
I simply help them realize
That they already are
They are my friends, my second family
When they're troubled I empathize
When they're happy I rejoice
And when they die I grieve
And no one is the wiser
For I am only the esthetician

The Artist

I put my paintbrush to canvas
Lost to the world around me.
I see nothing but the canvas,
It is a door to another dimension.
My brush and my paints
Are the lock and key.
From the very first stroke
The world around me disappears
And I am sucked into the vortex.
The vision in my head
Takes command of my hand
Feverishly jumping onto the canvas

Every stroke, every color know their place.
My eyes deceive me at times,
They panic for they do not see
What's in my head.
Frustration sets in and I fear I am lost.
But the vision takes command
Of my brush and my paints,
Forging ahead
To find it's new home on the canvas
Never ceasing till it's complete.
I am simply a vessel.
Each vision a passenger
Just passing through,
Guiding me to it's final destination
For all the world to see.

Passion

All consuming, irresistable,
It's what drives us to excel
And it can drive us crazy
Yet passion keeps us sane when life is crazy
Artists, musicians, thespians and writers
Are said to have it coursing through their veins
Passion multiplies every sentiment tenfold
If you try to bury it
It will fester
Eventually consuming you
Untill the only sentiment left is misery
If passion be your master,
Follow it till the end of days
Love will be ecstacy
Pain will be excrutiating
And life will be worth living

Intent

Our reason for being,
Our path in life,
What our soul intended to accomplish in this lifetime.
Each of us has our own intent.
It is usually very clear to us as children.
As we grow and come into adulthood
It is clouded by outside influences;
A parent's good intentions,
The general pessimism of others.
We must then begin the journey to find ourselves,
To once again feel comfortable in our own skin.
Dreams are often the answers to our questions.
When someone is passionate about their work,
They have found their intent.

When we can picture a beautiful path ahead,
And simply the thought of it
Makes our heart race,
And our soul shouts for joy,
We know we have found our intent.
When nothing can possibly feel more right,
Be more exciting
Yet give us complete peace of mind,
We have found our intent.
No matter how drastic a change there must be made
To acheive our individual goals and dreams,
Let nothing or no one hold us back
Including our own fear.
And let us remember that we are never alone;
God will always help us find and acheive our true intent.

Believing

There is nothing more powerful than a belief
Whether thought, spoken, or acted out.
We are all what and who we truly believe we are.
Did you ever notice
That people who always claim to be lucky
Always are?
People who believe they are truly blessed
Seem to have a never-ending amount of blessings
Thrust upon them?
Like happens when someone clings to the idea
That life is one hardship after another.
Is it so difficult to make the connection?
Who is right?
The optimist or the pessimist?
Both claim to be realists
Both are;
Their reality is what each believe it to be.
The universe will surround you with what you believe.
If you wish to change negative beliefs to positive
Count your blessings before you start your day
Count them again before you sleep
No matter how great or small
As the days pass, your blessings will grow
Both in number and in size
Till your life is filled with blessings
And you believe it always will be.

Music

It comforts the weary,
Soothes the downtrodden,
And calms us when we're stressed.
It's an expression of our innermost thoughts,
A celebration of emotions.
It is not only my release
But one of my passions,
Indeed one of my greatest loves.
It is the color of life.
Music is often the key to understanding each other;
Voicing thoughts that everyone can relate to,
Therefore uniting us
On a deeper level than any other means,
Virtually instantaneously.
It erases selfdoubt
By validating our innermost feelings.
To the musician it can only be described as
An emotional orgasm;
The energy that it generates
Is nothing short of addictive.

Travel

The greatest education comes from traveling.
It is easier to remain ignorant
And harbor prejudice
When you limit yourself
To your own little corner of the world.
Experiencing different cultures
Helps us understand
That we may have different customs
And ways of life
But we really are all
Part of a greater whole.
Traveling opens our hearts and minds
Leaving our cares behind.
It enables us to once more
Be able to see the world
Through the eyes of a child,
With wonderment and awe.
It renews our spirit
And helps us truely appreciate
Our own little corner of the world
And everyone in it.

Chapter Six : What I've Learned

Health

The most precious possession we have
Yet most take it for granted.
We eat too much,
We don't eat enough,
We eat food that poisons us,
And we eat at the wrong time
Knowing we are drastically lowering
Our quality of life.
We spend unimaginable amounts of money
To create foods that kill us
And we spend ridiculous amounts of money
For the privilege of eating it.
We seem to thrive on stress
Which kills us even faster
And also drastically lowers
Our quality of life.

It seems only when we are faced with death
Whether our own, our loved one,
A friend or aquaintance's,
Do we begin to realize how precious
Our health really is.
Without it we are nothing but miserable
Choosing slow suicide.
And yet all we need to do to stay healthy
Is to eat properly,
Stay calm,
And get active.
These three actions
Have the power to improve
Every aspect of our lives
Mind body and soul

Patience

Patience is the art of waiting without angst
The ability to carry on with other activities or thoughts
While anticipating the outcome of a certain event
Learning to see the beauty in life
Instead of being irritated by it
It is appreciating every moment,
Enjoying every task,
Knowing that life is eternal
So what's the hurry?
The more we try to rush
The less we are able to accomplish.
If we follow the ebb and flow of the universe
It will carry us to where we want to be.
Patience is enjoying the journey

Realizing that the only time that exists
Is this very moment.
It is having peace of mind.
It is the by-product of wisdom,
The child of enlightenment.
If we are happy, we are patient
One cannot be found without the other
It is living without fear or anger
Which are two forms of the same emotion
It is loving ourselves and seeing ourselves
In each and every living being
Thus treating each other accordingly......
With Patience.

Judgement

Worry not what others think or do
For the universe will give what it receives.
Everything and everyone has a purpose
Just because we don't always understand
What that purpose is
Does not make it wrong.
Let us not anguish about what has happened
But realize instead
It is how we respond that is important.
Anger simply aggravates a situation.
Attempting to control something or someone
Limits and stifles opportunity and growth.
Differences might sometimes be perplexing
Yet we must realize there is no bad or good.
Observe these differences with wonderment.

We are not all expected to agree,
Simply to allow each other to be who we are
Without wanting or needing anyone
To conform to our choices.
Remember what was considered right or wrong
Has changed many times
And will continue to change
Till we accept that there is no right or wrong.
Yet understand that there are consequences
To each action.
We must simply decide where we want to be
Then take the appropriate actions.
Accept that others may not choose the same path.
We can change the world
By being true to ourselves we become leaders
People will follow freely
Discovering their own true paths.

Confidence

We are encouraged to love ourselves
Yet when we do
We are deemed vain, conceited, or arrogant
We are told self confidence is good
Yet having it is a sin
We shouldn't compliment each other
For fear of a swelled head
If we feel good about ourselves
We must feel we are better than others
If we adorn ourselves with beautiful clothes or jewelry
We are considered shallow
If we work too hard to better ourselves
We are selfish and egotistical
If we work too hard to help others
We are accused of being fanatical
If we are to follow these standards
How can we be confident?
To be confident we must rebel
Against all of these stereotypes
Love ourselves mind, body and soul

Being confident is knowing we are worthy of love
So let us be vain
Let us be arrogant
Let us feel beautiful inside and out
It is then that we will notice the beauty in others
Everyone is worthy of love
Some of us just don't know it
Confidence can be contagious
Those of us who are blessed with an abundance
Should share it with those who are lacking
Compliment total strangers
Watch as their souls are uplifted
Life is not a burden
Confidence gives us wings
Enabling us to enjoy life to the fullest
Giving confidence to someone who has none
Helps them take flight
Giving everyone the strength to soar to new heights.

<u>Responsibility</u>

What will happen if I say this?
Who will be affected if I do that?
How will my life be changed?
The questions are the answers.
If we don't ask them
We choose to re-act.
To sleepwalk through life
Repeating the same actions.
The questions give us power.
Choosing how we behave in any given situation
Is having total control of our own lives
Who wouldn't want that?
The possibilities are endless;
The benefits immeasurable.
Responsibility is not a burden
It is an opportunity to excel.

Honesty

Living in truth
Knowing that success achieved without honesty
Is simply a house of cards.
Truth gives us freedom to live without fear,
To stand naked before the world
Having nothing to hide
Knowing all that separates us is an illusion.
No harm can come to us
Honesty gives us foresight
To recognize obstacles in our path
Enabling us to avoid them whenever possible,
Or prepare ourselves to overcome them.
Living in truth is the path to joy.
It gives us peace,
It is the only way of discovering who we are,
Of realizing who we want to be.
Honesty is reality.
It is simplicity.
It is not voicing opinions uncalled for;
An opinion is not necessarily the truth.
It is being our true selves,
Allowing each other to do the same.
With honesty we experience true love.

Hope Versus Fear

Don't get your hopes up for fear of disappointment
Expect the worst and hope for the best
Fear is a form of misery
Hope is a form of joy
Why be miserable from the very beginning
Even if the conclusion is disappointment
If you have hope you have joy till the very end
How is it possible to fear the worst,
Leaving you in total misery,
Yet simultaneously hope for the best
Giving your heart warmth and joy?
One cannot be an optimist
And a pessimist at the same time
Both misery and joy are contagious
You must choose
Which you prefer to surround yourself with.
Fear breeds violence, hate, and depression
Causing us to stagnate mentally and spiritually
Hope brings with it love and joy
The three give enlightenment

Money And Power

Money is not sinful or filthy
Just as Power is not corrupt
They are two of God's greatest gifts
They can be used to bring world peace,
Illiminate poverty and hunger,
Cure disease
As well as save our planet's ecology.
Unfortunately we have allowed these wonderful blessings
To fall into corrupt hands
Money can buy happiness
Power can do good
We are given both
We must simply choose how we are to use them
To help others and better ourselves,
Or waste them and achieve nothing
Allowing the corrupt all the control
The time has come for money and power
To serve their original purpose
The power is within us
With it, the money will follow

Laughter

The most beautiful, most joyous moments of life.
It is able to soothe the downtrodden,
Comfort the lonely,
And cure any ill when born of a loving soul.
The fountain of youth is within us.
Laughter is it's secret elixir
Children bathe in it at every opportunity
We as adults all too often forget its value
Not knowing how to quench our thirst
Yet some of us, though time passes on,
Remain forever young;
We remember that laughter cleanses the soul
Children are like the fruit of the vine;
Without laughter, they wither and return to seed
Only with love and laughter can they truly flourish
Without love, laughter is empty and cruel
A hollow imitation of a feeling
That instantly fills our souls with joy
Laughter born of love is pure ecstacy
It is the closest to nirvana we come to
On what should be a daily basis
In that very moment
Life as we know it is bliss

Success

There is nothing more individual
For it matters not how grand or how modest
Your goals are
If you accomplish what you set out to do
You are successful
There is nothing more unifying
There is no greater success
Than coming together to accomplish a commun goal
No special talent is required
Each person born can choose to be successful
Faith, confidence, and persistance create success
Have many goals
Yet focus only on one at a time
Be tenacious
Be patient
Remember always to enjoy every moment of the struggle
For misery never breeds success

Perfection

The most misused word in the english language.
There is nothing more subjective,
Especially when describing beauty.
What was considered perfect beauty centuries ago,
Or even only decades ago,
Has gone full circle many times over.
Whether describing inner or outer beauty,
Opinions of what is considered perfection for either
Have experienced a complete reversal many times.
Full figured or thin,
Submissive or strong and independant,
All have described the perfect woman
At one time or another.
Men have been subjected to equal scrutiny;
Having once been expected to be
Big, strong, rough and in charge,
Now are required to be
Gentle, understanding,
And immaculately groomed.

As cliche as it might sound,
The saying "Everyone is perfect in their own way"
Is the only statement that rings true.
However people are most critical of themselves;
I always say 'Don't beat yourself up,
There's a line up of people around the block
That will do it for you'.
Just because something or someone is not to your liking
Doesn't mean they're not perfect;
You simply have different preferences.
Everyone and everything is perfect,
Each having their own place
And purpose in the universe.
Just because we don't understand why
Doesn't make it flawed.

Chapter Seven : Dawn Has Broken

Waking From The Nightmare

How strange it is when life is wonderful
And yet the world around you is in turmoil.
When everyone around you is troubled
And your life is finally on track,
Dawn has finally broken.
Just when you thought you'd died and gone to hell
The nightmare is over.
But you wonder what is real;
This wonderful life you have now,
Or the darkness you just woke up from.
You're so happy you almost feel guilty
Because those you hold dear are in misery.
Just when you accept the fact
That all you ever had were just pipe dreams,
Along comes the Piper.
Just when you're about to crash,
Everything falls into place.
It feels like walking on water.

Why Me

Without a doubt the question
We ask ourself the most.
We become so self-absorbed
Those around us disappear,
And all that exists
Is ourself and our problems.
The universe, God or Satan,
Must be making all this happen
To test us, to bait us, or teach us a lesson.
Yet if we stop for just a minute
Our arrogance would be evident.
Why would any of these occurrences
Be exclusively about one person?
What purpose would it serve?
And what makes one more important than another
To deserve to be the center of all this attention?
We are each an equal and significant part
Of an unimaginably greater existence.

This is the greater lesson;
That each and every one of us
And every living thing,
Has an equally important role
Creating, sustaining and improving
The quality of life in our precious universe.
The question is therefore not "Why me?"
Rather "What can I say or do
To be a positive influence and contributor
Today and everyday?".
Why me?
Because every thought,
Every spoken word,
Every action or in-action,
Is a choice that has consequences
That effects countless

Time

Much is said about time;
Too much, too little,
Too fast, too slow,
Racing against it,
Never enough of it.
Time is precious,
Time is wasted.
Although it seems to stop
When soulmates connect.
The world slips away,
Such as it does
At the time of loss.
When your life gets wiped away
In the span of a heartbeat.
Time stands still,
For you cannot imagine
Life without your loved one.

Although time heals all wounds,
Painful times seem never-ending.
Yet it is well known
That it flies by in times of joy.
Truth be known,
Regardless of how you spend your time,
Whether elated or in misery,
Time is not cruel,
It is simply relentless.
It is completely unbiased.
So remember the past,
Be poised for the future,
But make the most of the present.
It's the only time we really have,
And it shapes both our memories
As well as our future.

Awakened

Throughout the years I've tried to grow,
To learn from each experience,
To be the person I knew I was capable of being,
To listen to my conscience, my instinct,
To understand myself so I could better understand others.
I learned empathy and patience,
Forgiveness and acceptance,
Yet despite my best efforts
There was still a missing piece.
I was still a prisoner of my own frustration.
I thought of every challenge as an obstacle,
I thought of every move I made,
I thought non-stop in fact.
As positive as I tried to be,
I still had to try to be positive
The answer came from a man named Tolle;
I am awakened to "A New Earth"
I am not my demons 'Ego and Pain',
No longer do they hold me prisoner.
I am not thought or emotion,
But the glorious peace when neither are present.
The freedom I was searching for was always within me.
I'm happy to say I'm awakened and out of my mind!
It was too crowded in there,
And I didn't like the company anyway.

New Beginnings

They can be both exciting and frightening
But there is no need to fear
It is an opportunity to create life anew
Fear is simply a wall
Preventing us from seeing the wonders before us
New beginnings impassion the soul
We are challenged to discover ourselves
Without competing against each other
New beginnings create experience
Experience gives wisdom
Wisdom leads to enlightenment
Enlightenment creates new beginnings
Embrace every day as an opportunity
Be excited about life
For it is the constant new beginning
Life is new beginnings in perpetual motion
They help define who we are
For we are forever changing
It is the soul's purpose
To experience new beginnings.

Chapter 8: Faith and Philosophy

Faith

To have no fear
To have no doubt
To know unquestionably that God always provides
All that is expected of Him
Asking for all your heart's desires without inhibition
Knowing that God's soul purpose for you in life
Is to experience Joy
Feeling you are never alone
Just as your heart is an important part of you
Feeling you are an important part of God
Knowing that everything God creates is perfect
In it's own way....
Including you.

Free Will

God said "I give you free will.
Never shall I renege on this Promise."
And so the human race chose it's path.
We chose to have war.
When there was much death and suffering
We said "God please end this"
And God said "I cannot"
"It was your choice to create war
You must choose to end it"
"I can only give you the strength to endure it"
Then we chose to create disease.
When there was much death and suffering
We said "God please cure us"
And God said. "I cannot"
"It was your choice to create disease
You must choose to cure it"
"I have already given you the means to do so"

We also chose to ravage our planet's ecosystem
When over half the species of plants and animals
Were extinct,
When we jeopardized the very air we breath,
The ground we walk on,
And the water we need to survive
We said "God we no longer want free will"
"Please tell us what to do"
And God said "I cannot"
"Never shall I renege on my Promise of Free Will"
"But if you gather together in my name
You shall have the power to change the world"
"Time is of the essence"
"You can no longer sit idly by
While the few destroy the many"
"The choice is your own, it always was."

Reincarnation

Reincarnation is eternal life
The evolution of the soul
We return repeatedly
To experience every aspect of life imaginable
Choosing to forget the knowledge of the universe
Time and time again
In order to experience life
Through the eyes of a child
With wonderment and awe
Each life seeing and feeling
Something different than before
It is not enough simply to know who we are
Our soul needs to experience who we are
Whether that be darkness or light
Though we each have the knowledge of enlightenment
We cannot experience being enlightened
Unless we first experience being ignorant

Each soul chooses it's own path
Each path is different from the other
We may choose the same repeatedly
Or progress rapidly
In our quest toward enlightenment
Being conscious of this
Means respecting another's choice of path
For each soul has a reason
Why we choose to be who we are
In this lifetime and the next
And each life has a purpose
That connects us all as one
When we decide to evolve consciously,
Taking responsibility
For our own words,
Thoughts and actions
In relation to all that is,
So that we may once again experience
The true Glory of God,
The joining of all souls,
The re-membering of the universe.

Surrender

To realize our desires, our goals,
We must try not to control them
We must try not to make things happen
Nothing can be accomplished alone
We cannot take something from the universe;
The universe will give of itself readily
If we surrender to it's power,
God's power.
Surrendering is not giving up our dreams,
It is a pleasant means of achieving them.
It is having desires, goals, and ambitions
And trusting God's universe to fulfill them.
It's consciously free-falling through life;
At first it can be frightening
But soon, it becomes exhilarating.
God speaks to us
Surrendering is learning to listen.

The universe guides us
Surrendering enables us to see where it is leading us.
Synchronicity is our never-ending source of opportunity
Surrendering allows us to recognize and appreciate it.
Surrendering is living without fear or stress.
It is choosing to be happy.
It is enjoying every moment.
It is realizing we are all one.
Separating ourselves from each other and God
Is like cutting off a finger;
The finger can accomplish nothing
If it is not with the body.
Surrendering is working with and as a part of....
The Body, ...
The universe, ...
God.

The Equation

Listening is said to be a gift
Patience is said to be a virtue
Only those who have neither agree
There is nothing commun about commun sense
Describing any sense as commun is devaluing it
Listening is a learned skill
Remaining silent requires self-discipline
Patience is born from empathy
Empathy is aquired through listening
Wisdom and understanding are the result of patience
The benefits of self-displine are wisdom and
understanding
Happiness is the peace of mind achieved
When attaining all of these
And having the sense to realize it.

Creation And Evolution

The great debate
As old as time itself
Was the universe created in less than a week?
Did millions of years elapse from beginning to end?
Both are true
Both are false
It is the Divine Paradox
The misconception being
That time is linear
A thousand years is but a day
A day can last forever
The truth cannot be heard with mere words
For language spoken
Cannot describe what is felt or envisioned
How are we to understand with words
That time does not exist?
Past, Present and Future
Are constant yet concurrent.
Evolution is the process of creation
The reverse may also be said
The simple truth being
That evolution is God's greatest creation.

Enlightened

Knowing we are a each a part of one whole being;
Like an atom is part of a molecule,
A molecule is part of a cell,
And a cell is part of a body.
We are all an intricate part of our planet
Which is a part of our universe
And everything is a part of God.
God is energy;
He is the atom and the mountain,
He is the universe and beyond,
He is each of us.
We need not pray for eternal life,
Energy never ceases
It simply changes form.
Each individual is bonded together as one
With everyone and everything.
The universe will give us what we give it.
When we choose to be loving with everyone,
We are loved by all.
When we choose to be giving all ways,
We receive endless riches.
Knowing all this,
Knowing there is no being that is unworthy,
Living this truth in thought, word, and action,
Is being enlightened.

And The Meek Shall Inherit The Earth

There are those who would like us to believe
They possess great strength
When in truth they are the great pretenders.
Hiding behind bold and crass behavior,
Trying to disguise the emptiness and fear,
Lashing out at anyone who threatens
To reveal their true nature.
They interpret aggression for strength,
And meekness for weakness.
The difference is the weak shall cower
When the angry beat their chest,
The meek will simply walk away
Leaving them without an audience.
The best revenge for anyone that has wronged you
Is to lead a good and happy life.
Peace of mind is our ultimate reward.
Anger and fear cannot dwell in a peaceful soul.
The greatest leaders have been the meek;
Mother Theresa, The Dalai Lama,
And Mohamet Ghandi
The aggressors shall always perish in shame
And the meek shall inherit the earth
For they lead by example
And they exemplify what everybody truly wants
A peaceful and joyful soul.

Strength

True strength is not physical.
True strength is the quiet dignity one displays
When facing lifes many challenges,
Always finding a bright side
When surrounded by darkness,
Never giving up
Knowing this too shall pass.
Life goes on with or without you.
Having strength is not only enduring it,
But enjoying the ride.
Even in the direst of circumstances
Being grateful still
For the love that surrounds you,
For all our blessings great and small.
Being able to recognize
That our greatest pain
Is also a blessing
For it's what gives us strength.
Without pain we do not grow
Either in strength or wisdom.
Pain teaches us appreciation;
If we do not appreciate every part of our lives,
The pain as well as the joy,
We have neither dignity nor strength.

Chapter Nine : Good Wishes

Christmas

Just one day each year
We get together with those we hold dear
To celebrate love and hope
And a man who represents both.
He told us we are all God's children
Regardless of race or beliefs.
It's a comforting thought to know
That God loves us all
No matter what we believe,
No matter what we call Him,
Or what language we speak.
Christmas celebrates the belief
That we are all equal,
That we are all loved,
And if only once each year,
We take time to appreciate
The people in our lives
That inspire us to love and hope.
We realize that all our toils,
And tribulations in our daily lives,
Are worth the effort.
So Merry Christmas to all!
For in God's eyes,
We are all his loved ones.

A New Year's Wish

May we all remember the year that has past;
Be proud of surviving the worst of it,
Learning from both trial and error,
Treasuring the laughter,
Forgiving ourselves for not accomplishing
All that we'd hoped to,
Getting satisfaction from that which we did.
The new year brings hope,
Always striving higher.
May we be healthier, calmer, and wiser.
Most important of all,
May we recognize the blessings we already have.
And when all seems grim,
There's always a new year to start over again.

Intuition

It is the voice of reason
It is the voice of God
It's that nagging little feeling we get
It's our Guardian Angel whispering in our ear
Some of us are very attuned to it
Some of us choose to ignore it
Many don't recognize it
It can be a fleeting thought
Or a clear vision
It is here to guide us
Protect and enlighten us
If we open our hearts completely,
Though we think by doing so we risk everything,
We are in truth, never more secure.
It is only then that intuition will lead us
To our full potential.
It is our soul telling us our purpose for being
Only by listening shall we discover our intent
Only by following our intuition
Shall we find fulfillment and joy.
Everything happens for a reason
Sometimes we don't know why
Our intuition gives us the answers.

Charity

Selfless giving,
Volunteering to help,
Whether it be family or friend,
Local or global,
It grounds us.
We are too often pre-occupied
With our daily tasks;
Charity reminds us to slow down
And appreciate our true reason for being:
To work together to improve the quality of life
Of each and every one of us.
We connot progress
If we do not work together.
It brings balance to our world;
Each of us have something valuable to contribute
Whether it be money, time, talent or strength,
We are all needed in some way.
Charity teaches us humility.
It helps us break the perpetual motion of stress
Because when we give
We are inundated with a feeling of peace and joy.
Charity gives us a sense of worthiness,
And isn't that what we're all searching for?

LaVergne, TN USA
24 September 2009
158963LV00003B/29/P